A Note to Parents and Teachers

SAINSBURY'S READING SCHEME is a compelling new reading programme for children, designed in conjunction with leading literacy experts, including Cliff Moon M.Ed., Honorary Fellow of the University of Reading. Cliff Moon has spent many years as a teacher and teacher educator specializing in reading and has written more than 140 books for children and teachers. He reviews regularly for teachers' journals.

Beautiful illustrations and superb full-colour photographs combine with engaging, easy-to-read stories to offer a fresh approach to each subject. Each book in the SAINSBURY'S READING SCHEME programme is guaranteed to capture a child's interest while developing his or her reading skills, general knowledge, and love of reading.

The five levels of the programme are aimed at different reading abilities, enabling you to choose the books that are exactly right for your child:

Yellow Level – Learning to read
Green Level – Beginning to read
Gold Level – Beginning to read alone
Ruby Level – Reading alone
Sapphire Level – Proficient readers

The "normal" age at which a child begins to read can be anywhere from three to eight years old, so these levels are only a general guideline.

No matter which level you select, you can be sure that you are helping your child learn to read, then read to learn!

LONDON, NEW YORK, MUNICH,
MELBOURNE AND DELHI

Editor Dawn Sirett
Art Editor Jane Horne
Senior Editor Ros Walford
Senior Art Editor Diane Thistlethwaite
Production Melanie Dowland
Picture Researcher Angela Anderson
Jacket Designer David McDonald
Natural History Consultant
Theresa Greenaway

Reading Consultant
Cliff Moon, M.Ed.

This edition published in 2011
First published in Great Britain in 2000 by
Dorling Kindersley Limited
80 Strand, London WC2R 0RL
Penguin Group (UK)

2 4 6 8 10 9 7 5 3 1
001–KP844–Jun/11

A CIP catalogue record for this book is
available from the British Library.

ISBN 978-1-4053-7562-7

Colour reproduction by Colourscan, Singapore
Printed and bound in China by L. Rex Printing Co. Ltd.

The publisher would like to thank the following for
their kind permission to reproduce their photographs:
Key: a=above, c=centre, b=below, l=left, r=right, t=top

Ardea London Ltd: Peter Steyn 4 bl; **Bruce Coleman
Collection Ltd:** Trevor Barrett 6–7, 19 c, Erwin & Peggy Bauer
28, Fred Bruemmer 10 t, Alain Compost front cover, 17, Peter
Davey 26 b, Chrisler Fredriksson 27 cl, 32 crb, Janos Jurka 22 t,
Steven C. Kaufman 15 t, 15 cr, 32 bl, Gunter Kohler 16 c, Stephen
Krasemann 24 b, Leonard Lee 7 t, Joe McDonald 3 b, 23 b, M. R.
Phicton 4 cra, 4 cr, Jorg & Petra Wegner 5 b; **DK Images:** Whipsnade Zoo,
Bedfordshire stickers tr; **NHPA:** B. & C. Alexander 12 b; **Oxford Scientific
Films:** Martyn Colbeck 9 t, 30–31 b, Daniel J. Cox 14 tr, 14–15 b, 32 clb,
Kenneth Day 5 tr, 13 t, 32 tl, Michael Fogden 13 b, Zig Leszczynski 10 b;
Planet Earth Pictures: Gary Bell 29 c, 29 inset, 32 br, Tom Brakefield
21 t, Robert Franz 25, M. & C. Denis Huot 2 br, 18 b, Brian
Kenney 27 t, Pavlo de Oliveira 8–9 b, Doug Perrine 20–21 b.

Additional photography for DK:
Peter Anderson, Jane Burton, Frank Greenaway,
Colin Keates, Dave King, Bill Ling and Tim Ridley.

Discover more at

Sainsbury's
Reading Scheme

Green Level
Beginning to read

Wild Baby
Animals

Written by Karen Wallace

Animals grow up in different ways.
They have lots of lessons to learn.
Some are born helpless but
their mothers protect them.

A newborn kangaroo is the size
of a bee.

She crawls
into her
mother's
safe pouch.

She doesn't open
her eyes for at least
five months.

eye

A newborn monkey cannot walk.
He is carried by his mother.

Other baby animals
can walk soon after they're born.
They learn to run
with their mother
when danger is near.

Baby rhinos stand on their hooves
a few minutes after
they are born.

hooves

A baby zebra can run
an hour after she is born.

Some baby animals are born
in a place that is safe.
Other baby animals are born
in the open.

Baby wolves are born in a cave.

A baby elephant is born
on open, grassy land.

Other elephants
make a circle
to protect her.

All the animals in this book
drink their mother's milk.
They are called mammals.

A seal's milk is fatty and rich.
Baby seals need lots of fat
to keep warm in the snow.

Baby bears
suck milk
for six months.

Baby elephants suck milk
for two years or more!

All baby mammals
stay by their mother
to keep safe.

On land, a baby walrus
stays tucked under her mother.

A baby kangaroo is carried
in his mother's pouch.

A baby sloth has to hold on tight.
Her mother is upside down!

Baby animals
must stay clean
to be healthy.

tongue

A mother cheetah
licks her cub's soft fur
with her rough tongue.

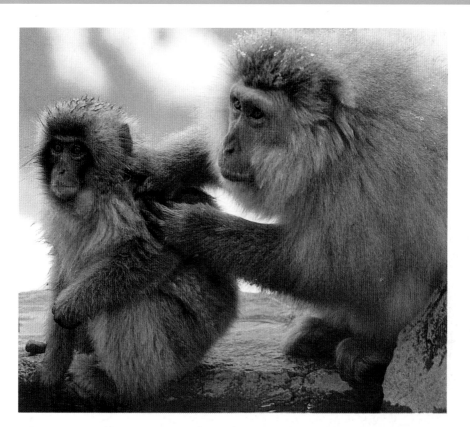

A monkey picks lice
from her baby's back
with her long fingers.

fingers

As baby animals grow
they need solid food.

Lion cubs eat
what their mother can catch.

Baby orang-utans
eat fruit
that their mother
has chewed for them.

Other baby animals
soon find food for themselves.

A baby buffalo
eats grass.

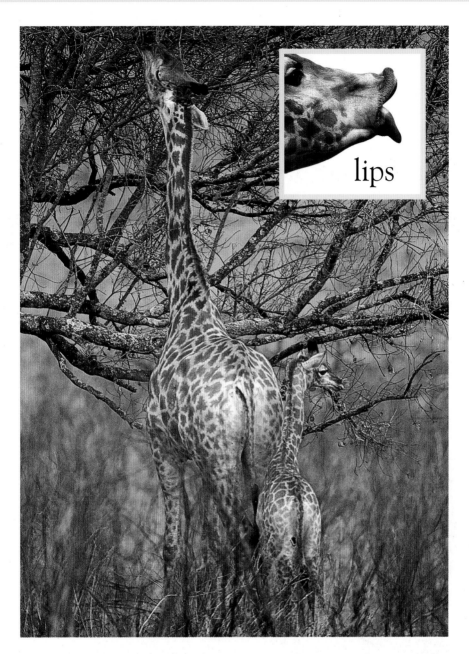

lips

A baby giraffe tears off leaves
with her thick lips.

Baby animals
know their mother's voice.
They find her quickly
if danger is near.

A baby dolphin
hears her mother
make a click-click-click sound.

CLICK!
CLICK!
CLICK!

A baby seal
knows her mother's bark. *ARRK!*

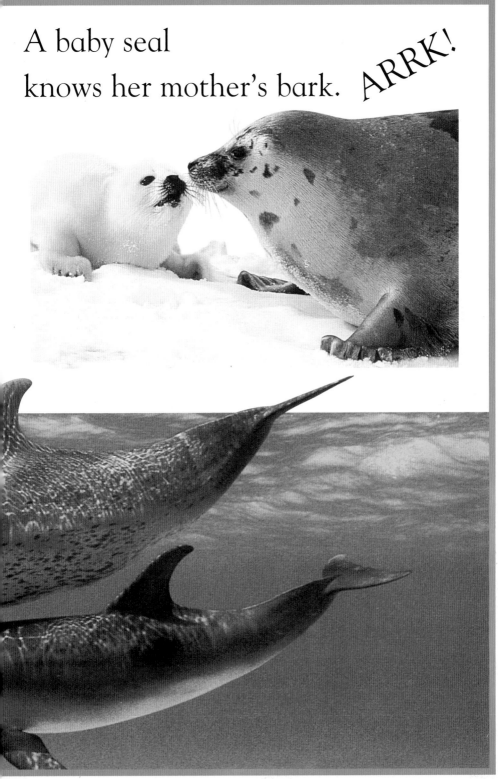

When there's danger in the water,
baby animals do as they're told.

Baby beavers dive
when they hear
the whack
of their
mother's tail.

tail

A baby hippo
stays with his mother
when she grunts a loud warning.

When there's danger
in the forest,
baby animals do as they're told.

A fawn lies still
in the grass
so she won't be seen.

Bear cubs
climb a tree
when their
mother growls.

As baby animals grow older
they start
to look after themselves.

A young chimpanzee
uses a stick to dig for insects.

Otter cubs learn to swim
so they can
catch fish.

trunk

A young elephant
uses her trunk
to rip leaves
from a tree.

Baby animals play games
that teach them how
to look after themselves.

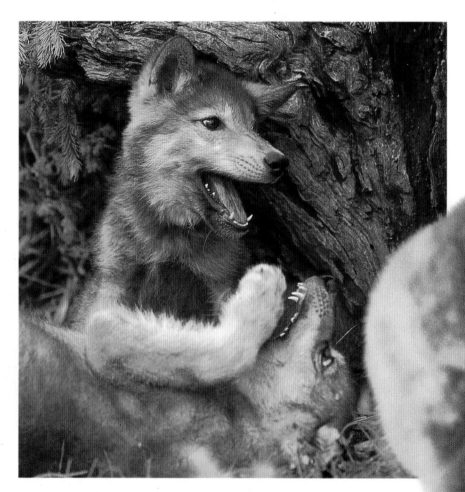

Wolf cubs wrestle and bite.
They're pretending to hunt.

Baby koalas play in the trees.
They're learning to climb
with their sharp claws.

claws

Baby animals grow up.
They learn their lessons well
and no longer need
their mothers.

Koalas are
fully grown
at two years.

Elephants are
fully grown
at twenty-five!

One day baby animals
are old enough
to have babies of their own.

Picture Word List

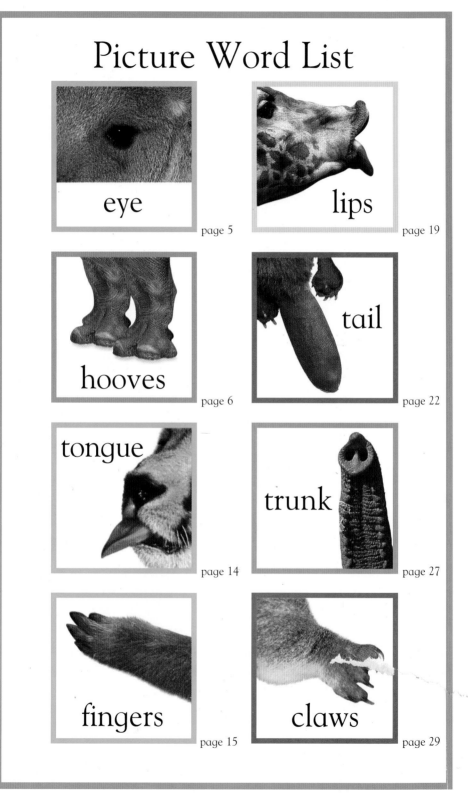

eye
page 5

lips
page 19

hooves
page 6

tail
page 22

tongue
page 14

trunk
page 27

fingers
page 15

claws
page 29